Senior Dogs: Tongues & Tales
"Love Lives Here"

We hope you enjoy this short collection of the Residents and Forever Fosters of House with a Heart Senior Pet Sanctuary

**Sherry Lynn Polvinale
& Jacqueline Raymo
Photos By Emily Renee Zea**

About House with a Heart Senior Pet Sanctuary

In 2006, Sher Polvinale and her late husband, Joe, created a senior pet sanctuary in their home. House with a Heart Senior Pet Sanctuary was founded to provide a forever home for dogs and cats who were either abandoned or given up by owners who could no longer care for them. Because of their age and various medical conditions, these senior pets had little chance of being adopted. Once a dog or cat became a resident, it had a loving home for life.

HWAH is a 501(c)(3) non-profit and our Director, Sher, devotes herself full-time to caring for the pets and maintaining and improving the Sanctuary. The Sanctuary is supported by volunteers from Montgomery County and the surrounding Metro areas. Our volunteers walk, bathe, and care for the residents, as well as clean and maintain the house and two-acre property. As of 2019, 55 dedicated volunteers had joined the HWAH family.

Our Mission:
The Sanctuary's Mission is to provide a "Helping Hand" for senior pets. For our residents, we are able to provide love, affection, and shelter, as well as medical care, such as diagnostic screenings, dental care, surgery, and medications, whatever is needed to provide them with a quality and comfortable life as long as possible.

Another way we help Senior and Special needs dogs is with our "K-9 Medical Miracles Grants". With this program we provide grants to participating Rescues when they agree to save a senior dog over 12 years from a shelter or an Owner Give-up. The majority of senior dogs who are given up have many medical problems and with these grants they can receive the medical care needed to make them comfortable and prepare them for an Adoptive or Forever Foster home.

We always encourage others to consider adopting or fostering a senior dog and our own Motto is "LOVE LIVES HERE"!!

Our Residents

Oh My Darling Clementine

*"Oh my darling, Oh my darling, **Oh my darling Clementine...**"*

On a cold and windy night in the middle of January 2016 our local shelter whisked 60 dogs away from a terrible life in a hoarding situation and brought them to safety. They immediately tended to their medical needs and began working on finding them good homes.

Clementine was one of the pups who suffered in this abusive home. She had a badly damaged back and crooked little hind legs that had never been cared for, and she was blind. Because of Clementine's special needs the shelter felt she would do best in our Sanctuary. We were thrilled to welcome Clementine to our pack.

Now Clementine lives the good life as she hangs out in the kitchen in her open pen area with her pottie pads and her little hut. She loves to snuggle inside her hidey hole and she especially loves it when our Vice President, Rich comes to visit. Clementine has bonded with Rich and every Saturday he drives over an hour from VA to the Sanctuary to spend time carrying Clementine around in his arms.

It is amazing how dogs like Clementine are so forgiving. Clementine has also adapted amazingly well to being blind. This little love can be set outside on the patio and will quickly find her way back inside, through the pet door, up the ramp and back into the kitchen. When she wants something she is VERY vocal and she has trained us all to come running when she calls. Those horrible days of neglect and pain are far behind her as all of us at HWAH make sure to remind her every day of how special and how loved she is.

Tinker - "Diminutive Dynamo"

Tinker's story is like that of many senior dogs abandoned and forgotten at a shelter when her people no longer wanted her.

This little girl came to HWAH, a true "Grumpy Gal" after being left at the shelter. As some would say "What do you expect?? She is a Chihuahua, after all" and who wouldn't be a little testy after being abandoned by her family.

With time, Tinker has become more and more engaged with people…. asking to be petted and running up to say hello. Her biggest complaint is when OTHER dogs do the same. She wants to be the only one!

Tinker is a powerhouse in a pintsized body…. She is a diminutive dynamo!! At 16 years old she is seven pounds of the three L's - love, lazy, and loud!! Tinker wants to be petted, snuggled and loved, but only on HER terms. She has no problem being picked up as long as you only touch her on the right side and only after 3 long strokes on her back. As always, do it her way or the highway!! A very serious Diva Dog this one!!!

One thing definitely NOT on her list of things to do – is to be examined by the Vet. Beware to anyone who tries to hold her steady… this is a feisty little Chihuahua, and she doesn't mind letting everyone know!! Tinker always makes us laugh and we love her more and more with each passing day.

Tinker

Wrigley - "Cute Combo"

Wrigley along with his Mom, Casey and his Dad, Pappy were dropped off at our local shelter when their people decided to move to Florida. Wrigley's Dad, Pappy, a little Papillon was quickly adopted leaving Wrigley and Casey at the shelter with no prospects for a loving home.

Wrigley and his Mom Casey joined the HWAH family and fit right in. Casey was plagued with severe Kidney Disease and passed in late 2018.

Wrigley is a cute combo of Min Pin and Pom. He is a lovely honey brown with black accents, big expressive eyes, ears that are constantly in motion keeping track of his surroundings, and a tongue that hangs out the side of his mouth that just goes on forever!!!

This easy-going pup gets along with everyone and if any other dog seems to have a problem with him he just moves off in another direction. He is quiet and calm until a meal is at hand and then he becomes quite animated, jumping and barking and insistent that he be first in line.

Wrigley is not a fan of being picked up, he isn't grumpy about it, just fearful. He does love when he gets the spa treatment, wiping off with a warm cloth, brushing, ear cleaning and face washing will bring out little groans of happiness from him and he will happily snuggle up in a lap for a long nap.

He doesn't see as well as he once did so when giving him a treat we have to make sure he sees his treat or he will lose it to one of his pack mates. Even then he is easy going and just looks confused about where his cookie might have gone.

Wrigley does have to wear a belly band as he has never seen a post, a pillar, a couch or chair that he doesn't feel is crying out to have HIS scent on it!! We laugh as he lifts his leg all around the house and when he looks up inquiringly we just tell him THAT is why he wears a belly band!!!

Happy - "But Maybe Grumpy Instead?"

Happy – it is sort of a misnomer as Happy would bring to mind a pup who is easy going, friendly and fun…. Oopsie – maybe his name should have been Grumpy????

Happy was once a fluffy white pup with his very own family and was much loved and pampered. Sadly one day he suddenly couldn't move his back legs…Happy's family tried to care for him but they were not equipped to give him the 24/7 care he needed.

When Happy arrived at HWAH, we went to work right away utilizing methods to make caring for him a bit easier.. He learned to wear a Belly Band to stay dry. We set him up in a tall baby crib so he could see everyone and be in the midst of all the activities. We bought him a fancy cart from Eddie's Wheels and he became mobile again.

Everyone loves Happy and wants to pet him and spend time with him… but over time he has become a little grumpy, and very particular about who he spends time with. He can be Happy one minute and Grumpy the next without warning!!! He gets along well with most of the doggie friends and he likes to lounge in his special spot on the couch or in his favorite chair. He moves in close for snuggles at bedtime with Sher and he is joyous when he sees Emily. When Greg comes for visits every other Saturday he loves to sit and watch sports with him. And we cannot forget that he loves his Mama Harriette who was our first VP at HWAH.

Some of this feisty pup's happiest moments are spent in his cart running in the yard, exploring and hanging out with his friends. In his cart he is once again mobile and free! Happy is an example of loving a dog just the way he is and making sure that we utilize the means and methods to keep him and others safe. We hope that he has a long and HAPPY life!!

Happy

Daphne - "Stealth Ankle Biter"

Daphne is a Stealth ankle biter when new people are around, but once she is your friend you are safe!

This darling blonde Chihuahua was rescued from a puppy mill and taken to the local shelter. Unfortunately, while in a foster home, she jumped off a chair and broke her leg. After surgery, she needed to be kept quiet and have 24/7 care so the shelter asked HWAH to provide a place for Daphne until she was healed and ready for adoption.

Of course, we all fell in love with this feisty pup and were sad when she left us to go to her new foster home to wait for adoption! A freak accident on her first day with her new foster family caused Daphne to break her leg AGAIN!!! When the consensus was to euthanize her we asked if she could instead come back and stay with us at HWAH.

With good medical care and several visits to the Orthopedic Specialist Daphne was able to walk again!! Her leg still looks a little odd but if you didn't know you wouldn't notice. Often Daphne dances on her hind legs in hopes of catching a treat.

Daphne surveys her HWAH Queendom from a comfy bed on the corner of the couch. From her perch she barks at anyone new who comes in and admonishes any doggies who might dare to play in front of her. She is one of the first in line when treats are being handed out….she is called Dancing Daphne for good reason!

In Chihuahua fashion she will sometimes do a stealth nip at the back of a leg when someone new is leaving the room so we try to always warn Newcomers to make friends with Daphne ASAP with treats in hand. I think this is all falling right in line with Daphne's secret plan!!!

Lucky Lady, Two BFF's for Jenny

A quiet senior Portuguese water dog mix sat in the corner of her kennel at the shelter. Her head hung down dejectedly and she avoided all eye contact. The pink slip on her kennel door indicated she was to be euthanized due to inability to interact. Thankfully, a visiting rescuer decided to give Jenny a second chance.

Jenny spent time in two different foster homes that were unable to rehabilitate a dog that was so emotionally shut down. In desperation they sent Jenny to HWAH to see if we could help. Since coming to the Sanctuary, Jenny has made progress. She will never be a gregarious and out-going pup but she enjoys spending time with those who accept her as she is. She has had the good fortune of becoming close friends with two other dogs during her time at HWAH.

Her first love was Buddy, a little Pug Mix who helped Jenny as she transitioned into her life at the Sanctuary. It was a sad time for Jenny when Buddy passed until Logan came along. Logan became Jenny's new Best Friend! Jenny loved to be next to Logan at all times. When Logan passed Jenny once again became a recluse, wanting to stay in her own quiet corner.

She does enjoy playtime with other dogs out in our big grass yard. We make sure that she has lots of opportunities to spend time with them. When you open the door she will rush out alongside her buddies, give a few joyous barks and run with her tail held high. All of our volunteers have made it their personal mission to give Jenny extra love and care. Loving her just the way she is.

Marvelous Marco

Marco was taken into the PG County Shelter as a stray. Poor pup was found all matted and limping with a toenail torn off of his bloody foot. At the shelter he was not a happy camper and tried to bite so things were not looking good for Marco. One of our volunteers learned about him and asked if we could take him in. Pet Connect Rescue decided they would pull Mr. Marco if HWAH could foster him. So our Team effort prevailed to save Marco.

Marco arrived at HWAH matted and dirty and with a horribly infected mouth. Our incredible Groomer Emese, gave Marco a soothing bath and a hair cut and turned him into a handsome fella. Dr. Smith and his team examined Marco and found that he needed ALL of his teeth removed. After his dental surgery and healing Marco felt so much better and had a new "leash" on life…. He went from a shy worried tail tucker to MARVELOUS MARCO!!!!! Now Marco is a HWAH Resident and will sit in any and all laps whether or not there is already a dog in the lap.

Marco Marco Marco – that is what you hear me constantly saying….. He thinks he is our Head Security Guard…. Anyone who moves and shouldn't (according to Marco) will be barked at…. If he hears a noise that no one else hears he will jump up immediately and be ready as if he has a Marvelous Marco cape on and off he will run – out through the pet door, up to the fence to bark and show that Marvelous Marco is on the way to save the day!!!!!!

 And you know what???? He is usually right!!! Someone might have just turned into the driveway, a delivery is being made in the receiving area, someone opened a door from the basement kennel area, or Rocky dared to get up from a nap and head out of his pet door in the foyer. Nothing and no one can escape Marvelous Marco!!!

Marlie - "With Attitude"

Marlie is a handsome Toy Australian Shepherd with attitude!!! He came to HWAH along with his housemate, Dixie (now passed) when the Sisters they had been living with for 10 years were being moved from their home base and they could no longer keep the pups. Marlie and Dixie were loved very much, and it was a difficult transition for the Sisters and the pups.

Marlie is not without his little quirks. I noticed that when it was his turn to come into the kitchen to eat his breakfast or dinner he was nowhere to be found. I would have to go out and call him and he would come running from the furthest corner of the yard, dash past me and run to the kitchen gate to get his meal. Now I realize that when he sees the meal prep he runs outside and begins his vigil…. He waits patiently until he hears me call him and then he flies through the pet door, and begins a crazy dance accompanied by high leaps and even higher pitched moans and barks as if he has never eaten before. It is quite an amazing ritual that he sticks to rain or shine!!

Another interesting quirk is Marlie's penchant for herding the other dogs. Originally, he tried to do that with people and would give a nip at the back of a leg to move a person over or hurry them along. He quickly learned that this was not an acceptable behavior, so he turned his talents to the other dogs. At first it was only Nora who would find herself being herded into another room or nipped and prodded to move aside. He has now added Tator to his list and will occasionally reach out to block a dog running up to receive a treat. He is quite serious about this job that he has taken upon himself, so we keep a close watch to make sure it does not escalate beyond his suggesting into his demanding the other dogs comply.

Coco the Bichon

Coco is a reserved little Bichon who prefers her own company most of the time. Coco's Owner loved her little pup very much, but sadly financial and health issues made it more and more difficult for her to give Coco the care she needed. When she reached out to us for help we were happy to offer Coco a home at HWAH and to welcome her Mom to come for occasional visits.

We were able to provide Coco the medical care she needed and as she recuperated from her surgeries we got to know her better. It seemed she wanted so much to be cuddled and loved but her shyness would always win out.

With time she finally allowed Sher to pick her up and bathe and brush and comb her. She still plays hard to get with most people but has let her guard down more and more as the months go by. When the Sanctuary is quiet she will often come for a sit down and cuddle with Sher and the other Resident pups. When someone new comes in she will run to find a quiet bed to hide in until the coast is clear.

Others are working on being accepted by this discerning pup. Chris, Emily and Lori have made great strides in earning her trust. They are not to be denied Coco Cuddles!!! We are looking forward to the day when Coco accepts all of us!! If that day never comes, we will love her anyway!

Coco

Rocky - "Kept Fighting, Round after Round"

Rocky was brought to us by BARCS, another local rescue, following an Animal Control violation by his original owners. His condition was absolutely heartbreaking and deplorable.

This poor pup was extremely emaciated and presented with a condition in both eyes that caused him irritation and much discomfort. He also had a small growth on his right eye, severe dental tartar, as well as a ruptured mass on his hind quarters. After helping him gain weight we were able to make arrangements for his needed surgeries.

To make sure Rocky continued to improve we signed him up for Physical Therapy Treatments. He had so many PT, massage and laser treatments that Lori, our Asst. Director had a magnetic car sign made for our transport volunteer, Frances that said "HWAH – Medical Transport". We should have made another sign that said "HWAH ANGEL". Frances often made 2 to 3 trips a week to the Vet with Rocky.

Because of this constant loving care we were able to celebrate when we received a message from our Vet, Dr. Handel, that Rocky needed to lose 3 pounds. We consider Rocky a true success story as he arrived at HWAH sick and so thin at 44 pounds and now he is a strapping 78 pounds of Happy dog!! Rocky especially loves his big red ball and his visits and walks with his Guardian Angel, Lisa. And we thoroughly enjoy laughing at his many silly sleep positions!

Tator - (aka Tator Tot)

Tator was another little pup who suffered in a hoarding situation. He was rescued by our friends at Pet Connect Rescue. Pet Connect thought that since Tator was not "housebroken" he might do better in the home-like setting at HWAH rather than having to be kept in a crate. We agreed to have Tator join the HWAH family.

Although a bit shy and anxious, Tator quickly settled in with the HWAH pack. This little pup enjoyed going out in the yards every few hours and hanging out with all of his pack-mates but was worried and shy around new people. With the passing of time he has seemed to settle in and get a better handle on his fear of people.

Tator is one of our younger residents at an estimated 8 years old, and he is still full of "Vim and Vigor". During outdoor playtime, while his older doggie pals are hanging out, Tator challenges his biggest enemy-his tail!! He will dart around in circles desperately trying to catch this elusive prey that seems to stay just one step ahead of him!!

Poor Tator's biggest fear is the vacuum…. No amount of cuddling or sweet talking can take his mind off of his fear of the dreaded vacuum so we have decided a broom will work just fine!!! Tator will always be a shy fellow but he is slowly coming out of his shell, showing us his entertaining and fabulous self. Slowly but surely, he has started venturing out when people arrive. He has even started to allow some people to hold him and pet him.

Tator has come a long way from the shy anxious dog who arrived at HWAH. He is such a sweet fellow and every day he becomes more confident and we are thrilled to see him thrive with our pack.

Sher's Joie

Joie is a Blue Black Standard poodle. She is our Director, Sher's very own dog and we are including her as she is truly a big part of House with a Heart.

In December of 2013 after the untimely death of Sher's beloved poodle Dolly who passed away from cancer, the volunteers led by our then Vice President, Harriette, made secret plans to make sure a standard poodle puppy came into the Sanctuary. They knew that a puppy might help to lift all of our spirits. We decided to name the puppy Joie – which means Joy in French and would also be a tribute to Sher's Joe. On December 28th, Joie arrived, transported by our dear friend Katie. There were lots of tears and many arms reaching out to hold the precious puppy!!

Now Joie is 5 ½ years old. She is a wicky, wacky, enthusiastic, animated, vivacious, crazy bundle of energy and high spirits. Joie has a volunteer Guardian Angel, Joan who comes each week to spend several hours just with Joie. Joie can barely contain her excitement when Joan arrives… she sneezes, shows her teeth in a huge grin, and turns crazy circles to show her delight in anticipation of Joan's undivided attention.

At the end of each day when the Sanctuary goes quiet, Sher finally gets a chance to sit and snuggle with Joie and reflect on the day, on the hard work of all the volunteers, and how eternally grateful she is for all of the loving people in her life and for the opportunity to be able to care for, and love, until the end of their lives so many wonderful senior dogs. Joie is a big part of that JOY!!

Piper - "Belle of the Ball"

Piper's beginnings were not very bright or hopeful. At 6 months old she was only 6 pounds and came to us for hospice care because she was not thriving. Her Vet had recommended euthanasia, but her Owner couldn't bring himself to let Piper go.

Our job was to love her for as long as we could and then let her go when she was no longer comfortable. It was touch and go in the beginning with lots of Vet visits, medications and special care as well as many frightening stays in the ER.

Everyone adored this sweet Beagle pup and once she began to experience the crazy love that everyone at the sanctuary had for her, not only did she begin to improve, but she blossomed!!

Piper is truly like the Energizer Bunny – she just keeps on going and going and going!!! She is full of beans and is animated, spirited and lively and when she is not bouncing around she is snuggling and giving licks and LOVE.

Who would have thought that this lethargic, barely responsive pup who arrived at HWAH wrapped in a blankie for Hospice care would end up being the Belle of the Ball, the Light of our Lives and a constant source of laughter and animation!!!

"Forever Fosters"

As you know, House with a Heart residents are dogs who come to HWAH and have a "Home for Life".

But SOMETIMES it is not the best of the best and that is what we always want for our charges.

Some pups become "Forever Fosters".

These are pups who are happier in a more calm and quiet setting with more hands-on care than they can get in the Sanctuary full of doggie friends all vying for attention.

Our Forever Fosters

Jamison (aka Jamie)

Jamison, a handsome Shih Tzu was among 60 dogs who were rescued from a hoarding situation one cold and windy January night in 2016. The dogs were quickly transported to our local County shelter where medical treatment was started immediately as many of the dogs were quite ill and in pain.

Jamison was suffering from an infected eye and a cancerous tumor on his chest. The shelter made sure that this quiet pup received all of the medical care he needed. Once he was recuperating from surgery to remove one eye and the tumor on his chest the shelter reached out to HWAH to ask if Jamie could join another senior dog rescued in the same raid. Little Clementine was already safely settled in at the Sanctuary and she remembered Jamison when he arrived! They greeted each other like old friends!

As time passed it seemed that Jamison was holding back and not really sharing his total personality. He was reluctant to leave his bed for fear another dog would take it while he was gone. We began to wonder if he would benefit from being in a Forever Foster home without such a large group.

House with a Heart is blessed to have so many incredible volunteers and one of them, Susan, had been spending a lot of time with Jamie. It was pretty easy to convince her to take him home for a weekend visit. That visit thankfully turned into a new Forever Foster home for Jamison. He thrived with the personal attention and the loving care of Susan and her husband Joe. This quiet unassuming dog now has an engaging and joyful personality and those days of wondering if he would have a bed to sleep in are over!!!

How Bear Worked His Magic

It was a cold November afternoon when we heard the doorbell ring.
A sad looking family stood at our gate holding a thin, scared 13 year old dog that they wanted to surrender. We explained that HWAH was full to capacity and just couldn't take him. They insisted that they had no other options, opened the gate, set the little dog down and turned and walked away.

Sher and Lori immediately brainstormed to figure out what to do to help this poor pup. He was so sweet and looked just like a fox! He was malnourished and his nails were so long they curled around making it hard for him to walk comfortably. Lori suggested we fix him up and foster him until we could find him a perfect home.

Lori had an ulterior motive as she was already smitten!! Her secret plan was to bring him to her house to foster, and ultimately keep him. The only obstacle would be her husband, John. She knew she needed John's approval.

She got the little guy home, and named him Bear. Bear being a clever little dog knew what to do so he immediately connected with John. John got down on the floor to say hello and Bear walked up to him and kissed his nose. Later that night, Bear snuggled in with John on the couch. The next evening, John said that Bear was his. Now, even though Bear also loves Lori, he follows John everywhere, cries when John leaves the house and stares at the door until he returns.

He was not a very active pup until his new Forever Foster sister, Poppy, arrived. At first he ignored her, but after a YEAR, he decided to start playing with her. From the moment these 14 year old doggies wake up, they romp, and play. It is so incredibly sweet to know that these 2 seniors have found happiness and love!

Bear

BooBoo - "Happy Days Indeed"

One night in 2016, I received an email appeal from a rescue in North Carolina.

A family had abandoned their little blind poodle at a shelter and the pup was not doing well. We had space available and plenty of love to give. I immediately sent out a call for help to transport BooBoo to House with a Heart, and Nancy, one of our beloved volunteers answered!! She met the transport from NC and brought the little guy right to our door.

It was evident that on the ride Nancy had fallen crazy in love with Mr. BooBoo, and before too long she became his Forever Foster Mom.

At first, BooBoo was barely able to walk down their driveway on a leash. He was anxious and trembled at every sound or wisp of wind in his face. In the house, he stayed in his bed and seemed afraid to move or venture out. He was unduly quiet. Nancy, and her husband Mark, were not to be undone by a little bundle of black fluff, so they continued to shower BooBoo with love and care.

With their constant affection and attention he finally came out of his shell. He can now bark with the best of them and can walk for a mile with his head and tail up and a big doggie smile on his face. Nancy says he would be faster if he didn't stop to sniff all the messages left by other dogs.

Happy Days INDEED!!

BooBoo

Gidget - (aka Lady Gidget)

Poor little Gidget could have easily been confused for a dirty lump of fur when she was found on the street in Baltimore. After a thorough grooming, an adorable little Lhasa Apso was revealed. Gidget quickly went into a great Foster Home, but circumstances changed and the Senior Dog Sanctuary of MD asked if Gidget could join our pack and we said YES!!

Although Gidget had been found as a stray it was guesstimated that she was about 12 years. Gidget has an incredibly laid back personality. It seems nothing at all bothers or ruffles her feathers. She is quiet and unassuming… a stoic pup who plods along for her daily walks while her forever foster brother, BooBoo skittles about like a water bug.

Nothing about Gidget is fast. All of her movements are calm and calculated for the least amount of exertion. Food, however will get her full attention!!

Gidget may be blind, but with guidance she is able to get around, even going up and down stairs and over and under obstacles. She walks well on her leash, although she is no aspiring track star!!

This little couch potato is happy to snooze the day away with her tongue peeking out, and would only be happier to do so with company on a nice comfy couch.

No more cold and dirty city streets for this old gal!!

Poppy - "Love Magnet"

Poor little Poppy !!! Another sad case of an elderly owner who had to go into a nursing home, and was left with no choice but to give up her little companion dog.

When we learned about this little poodle who was in trouble, we quickly made arrangements to bring her to the Sanctuary. She weighed only 4 pounds with much of her hair missing and rotting teeth. She looked like a little monkey with her crooked, bowed legs and funny, little expressive face. As usual, we gave Poppy all of the medical care she needed to feel good again, and of course, a grooming so she could show off her feminine side.

Poppy might be teeny tiny, but her personality is OH, SO BIG!! She definitely showed us her spunky nature right away. Everyone fell in love with all of that cuteness mixed up tight with her gutsy and spirited persona. To look at Poppy is to look at a LOVE MAGNET. You just can't help yourself – she is so engaging!

While all of us were falling in love with Poppy, Poppy was falling in love with our Asst. Director, Lori. No amount of attention from anyone else could pull Poppy's eyes away from Lori if she was in the room. If Lori was anywhere at the Sanctuary, none of us could get Poppy into her arms fast enough. How could such a teeny tiny creature make so much noise??? There was nothing else to do but have Lori become Poppy's Forever Foster Mom.

With her one little snaggletooth fang, Poppy is ruling the roost in her new home with Lori, John and their other HWAH Forever Foster dog, Bear. She is truly LOVED!

Poppy
Photo By Lori Whitehurst

Spike - "Favorite Hobby - Naps!"

Spike, formerly known as "Spice", a twelve year old hairy, hairless Chinese Crested came to the sanctuary after his owner passed away and her husband was taken to a nursing home. Spike was suffering from terrible acne and dry eye, conditions that are common with his breed. He was sporting a natural Mohawk hairdo that blew in the wind giving him a Fabio kind of look!

Although Spike quickly settled into the Sanctuary routine he was never entirely comfortable with all of the commotion. We knew we should be on the lookout for a great Forever Foster home where he would not have to share with so many other dogs and life might be a little less hectic.

Years passed and finally Spike's Princess Charming arrived, one of our new volunteers, Emily!!! She was his perfect match and he was IN LOVE. Thankfully, Emily felt the connection and returned his affection. We soon made arrangements for Spike to become Emily's Forever Foster pup.

Since Spike is hairless, he gets colder than a typical full furred dog, and is also susceptible to sunburn which is why he has an extensive wardrobe. He can usually be seen wearing a fancy sweater, a polo shirt, onesie or even a jaunty hat.

Emily says that Spike's favorite pastime is to take naps and that he has a very loud SNORE!!! He can wake up the whole house with his very impressive late night snores and snuffles. Spike is now living the good life. He is a pampered senior dog, often riding in his own stroller or in his favorite spot of all – in the arms of Emily where he will always feel safe, loved, treasured and at peace.

Sally - "An Amazing Transformation"

Some of the residents that have come to us over the years have been in really rough shape when they arrived- some were homeless, some were abused, and some were just plain neglected. Sweet Sally was all of those things!!

Sally is a case that shows the amazing transformative power of some good old-fashioned TLC and love. Our little Sally is estimated to be close to ten-years-old. This lovable, dear girl came to us as a severe neglect case and was given to us in deplorable condition. She was covered in dried urine and feces as if she had been left in a crate with no way out. She had bald spots where her hair was just peeling off of her skin. She was so thin we could count every rib. If ever a little dog needed the restorative powers of love and care it was Sally.

We are thrilled to report that Sally is now a thriving, happy and healthy little poodle living in her Forever Foster home with the one human she loves the most – Frances!

When Sally lived at the Sanctuary and Frances would come to visit us, Sally couldn't hide her delight and when Frances left the Sanctuary she couldn't hide her distress! Sally made it known in no uncertain terms that Frances was her person. Thankfully, Frances agreed and now Sally shares her love for Frances with her pack mates, Sage and Barkley.

Monroe - "Medical Miracle"

When our dear friend Rebecca, asked us to provide hospice care for a six-month old Chihuahua puppy who was very ill and likely had only a short time to live, our answer was a resounding YES!!

When he arrived, our hearts sank. The little guy was thoroughly helpless. He couldn't see. He could barely stand up. He would put his face in his bowl of food but not open his mouth and then whimper with frustration. We shed lots of tears….and then we got to work. Volunteers came every day to hold him and help syringe feed him.

Our friend Rebecca took Monroe to see a Neurologist and he went through many exhaustive tests. The diagnosis was that Monroe had been asphyxiated in some fashion to such an extent that many of his brain cells had died. If those cells regenerated he would get better and if they did not we would lose him.

Everyone who met Monroe adored him and I think we loved him to recovery as after a few weeks he slowly began to improve in every way. He just continued to get better and better until he didn't resemble in anyway the poor pitiful pup who arrived in such horrible condition.

Monroe became our Miracle Mascot, Best Friend to Piper, and eventually went to live with his Forever Foster Mom, Karen and his canine sister, Penelope. This match made in heaven had only one caveat – that Monroe would spend several nights each month at the Sanctuary so we can all bask in his wonderfulness.

Monroe

Our Kitties

Munchkin - "First Forever Foster"

One of our very first HWAH Forever Fosters was Munchkin who is now 10 years old.

Munchkin came to HWAH when she was found as a stray kitty. Since Munchkin only had 3 legs we wanted a special home for her.

When our friend Siggi lost her beloved cat of 19 years, Sweet Pea, she was interested in fostering a cat that would sit on her lap and keep her company. Munchkin was a perfect fit and went to live with Siggi in 2010.

Munchkin's Mom, Siggi, says that she loves to watch the birds in her backyard. She is a lively, loveable kitty that loves to sit atop her 3 tiered cat perch, in her bed in the front bay, or on the ledge of one of the back windows.

She gets all of the attention and love as the only cat and in return she adores her Mom and listens intently to every word she utters.

Munchkin
Photo By Siggi Kaeufer

Gianni - "Kitty Love"

Gianni is a kitty with a sweet personality and many fans at HWAH. He came to us years ago when a new member of his family had a terrible allergic reaction to him. It was a sad day for his family but a happy day for our Sanctuary as Gianni added much to our kitty pack. We were thrilled when some members of his family were able to visit with him over the years…so it turned into a win-win situation.

Gianni is such a stoic kitty and never was that more apparent than the day when he jumped up on a shelf to groom himself. When he jumped down to come for his dinner we believe his leg became caught and it snapped. I was calling him…kitty, kitty…and went to look to see what was taking him so long. He walked slowly towards me as if there was nothing unusual about having a leg that was swinging in a circle obviously horribly broken.

All he wanted was his dinner but you can imagine I was in a panic. It was so fortunate that our Vet, Dr. Neville just happened to be here that day. She was able to give Gianni immediate medical attention in her mobile Vet clinic. We hoped that his leg would heal and he would be fine, but it did not and eventually he had to lose his leg.

You would never know that he suffered this loss…he gets up on the kitty perches, on the bed and into any lap that is available. He does enjoy giving kitty love nips so you have to always be ready, but he means no harm.

"Boss Cat" - Fluffy

Fluffy was rescued as a tiny kitten when her Kitty Mom could no longer care for her. She was bottle fed and raised at HWAH

Fluffy — oh this is a kitty with an ATTITUDE!!!! Look out if you are intending to brush her. She is fast as lightening with her teeth and claws. She believes herself to be the Boss Cat and expects everyone to respect her personal kitty space.

For Fluffy, the higher the better and she loves her toys… the laser light is no match for her.

Fluffy is also a food connoisseur, canned, kibble or treats – they are all good and need to be served RIGHT NOW!!! She is a delicate eater that looks as if she needs a lace hanky to wipe her whiskers with.

Fluffy welcomes all volunteers to care for her needs as any Diva would with a bit of distain and sometimes allowing for some restrained affection.

It always makes me smile when a kitty volunteer reports that Fluffy was so sweet today… only on her terms – only on her terms!!!

www.ingramcontent.com/pod-product-compliance
Lightning Source LLC
Chambersburg PA
CBRC102059150426
43197CB00006B/112